Article 14

The Right to Freedom of Thought, Conscience and Religion

A Commentary on the United Nations Convention
on the Rights of the Child

Editors

André Alen, Johan Vande Lanotte, Eugeen Verhellen,
Fiona Ang, Eva Berghmans and Mieke Verheyde

Article 14

The Right to Freedom of Thought, Conscience and Religion

By

Eva Brems

Professor of Human Rights Law at the Human Rights Centre,
Ghent University, Belgium

MARTINUS NIJHOFF PUBLISHERS
LEIDEN · BOSTON
2006

This book is printed on acid-free paper.

A Cataloging-in-Publication record for this book is available from the Library of Congress.

Cite as: E. Brems, "Article 14: The Right to Freedom of Thought, Conscience and Religion", in: A. Alen, J. Vande Lanotte, E. Verhellen, F. Ang, E. Berghmans and M. Verheyde (Eds.) *A Commentary on the United Nations Convention on the Rights of the Child* (Martinus Nijhoff Publishers, Leiden, 2006).

ISSN 1574-8626
ISBN 90-04-14721-7

Cover image by Nadia, $1^1/_2$ years old.

http://www.brill.nl

PRINTED IN THE NETHERLANDS

CONTENTS

LIST OF ABBREVIATIONS

ACHPR	African Charter on Human and Peoples' Rights 1981
ACHR	American Convention on Human Rights 1969
ACRWC	African Charter on the Rights and Welfare of the Child 1990
CERD	International Convention on the Elimination of all forms of Racial Discrimination 1965
CFREU	Charter of Fundamental Rights of the European Union 2000
CRC	Convention on the Rights of the Child 1989
CRC Committee	UN Committee on the Rights of the Child
ECHR	European Convention on Human Rights and fundamental freedoms 1950
ECmHR	European Commission of Human Rights
ECtHR	European Court of Human Rights
EU	European Union
CCPR	International Covenant on Civil and Political Rights 1966
CESCR	International Covenant on Economic, Social and Cultural Rights 1966
CMW	International Convention on the protection of the rights of all migrant workers and members of their families 1990
UDHR	Universal Declaration of Human Rights 1948
UN	United Nations
UNESCO	United Nations Educational, Scientific and Cultural Organisation

AUTHOR BIOGRAPHY

Eva Brems (° 1969, Belgian) studied Law at the universities of Namur (candidat en droit, 1989), Leuven (licenciaat rechtsgeleerdheid, 1992), Bologna (exchange student 1991) and Harvard (LL.M 1995). She obtained a Ph.D. in Law from the University of Leuven (1999), with a dissertation on 'Human Rights: Universality and Diversity' (Martinus Nijhoff, 2001). Before joining Ghent University, she was a researcher at the university of Leuven (1992–1994 and 1995–1999) and a lecturer at the university of Maastricht (1999–2000). In Ghent, she is a part-time Professor of Human Rights Law, and a part-time research fellow of the Fund for Scientific Research – Flanders. Her research covers most areas of human rights law (Belgian law, European law, international law, comparative law). She is the author of numerous publications in this field in Belgian and international journals and books, and a member of the editorial board of several law journals. She is the chair of VORMEN (Flemish organisation for human rights education).

TEXT OF ARTICLE 14

ARTICLE 14	ARTICLE 14
1. States Parties shall respect the right of the child to freedom of thought, conscience and religion.	1. Les Etats parties respectent le droit de l'enfant à la liberté de pensée, de conscience et de religion.
2. States Parties shall respect the rights and duties of the parents and, when applicable, legal guardians, to provide direction to the child in the exercise of his or her right in a manner consistent with the evolving capacities of the child.	2. Les Etats parties respectent le droit et le devoir des parents ou, le cas échéant, des représentants légaux de l'enfant, de guider celui-ci dans l'exercice du droit susmentionné d'une manière qui corresponde au développement de ses capacités.
3. Freedom to manifest one's religion or beliefs may be subject only to such limitations as are prescribed by law and are necessary to protect public safety, order, health, or morals or the fundamental rights and freedoms of others.	3. La liberté de manifester sa religion ou ses convictions ne peut être soumise qu'aux seules restrictions qui sont prescrites par la loi et qui sont nécessaires pour préserver la sûreté publique, l'ordre public, la santé et la moralité publiques, ou les libertés et droits fondamentaux d'autrui.

CHAPTER ONE

INTRODUCTION*

1. As one of the classical fundamental freedoms, the freedom of thought, conscience and religion has been firmly entrenched for all human beings, most notably in Article 18 of the CCPR (*cf. infra*). Yet at the same time, it is not self-evident to recognize children as autonomous bearers of this right, since several international provisions recognize the right of parents and legal guardians to ensure the religious education of their children in conformity with their own convictions (Article 18(4) of the CCPR, Article 13(3) of the CESCR). Hence the religion of children seems to have been brought within the realm of the rights of their adult caretakers. As a result it is not clear to what extent Article 18 of the CCPR and equivalent provisions in other treaties (*cf. infra*) apply to children. Moreover, Van Bueren notes that religious freedom for children has always been a problematic issue in international law, and that in the context of the CRC, 'disagreement over the extent of the rights, as applicable to children, risked obstructing the drafting and adoption of the entire Convention'.[1] Therefore, as is the case for the other 'autonomy rights' or 'participation rights' in the CRC (Articles 12 to 17), the explicit recognition of children's freedom of thought, conscience and religion is significant as a recognition of children as autonomous subjects of law, despite the similar wording in earlier human rights provisions. Parental rights with regard to the religion of their children have not been set aside however, and are explicitly added in the second paragraph of Article 14. Yet the difference between this provision and the phrasings in other conventions further illustrates the paradigm shift operated by the CRC (*cf. infra*, No. 52 *et seq.*).

2. In most situations, Article 14(1) and (3) of the CRC will be interpreted in line with Article 18(1) and (3) of the CCPR. In that respect, reference will

---

* September 2004
[1] G. Van Bueren, *The International Law on the Rights of the Child* (The Hague, Martinus Nijhoff Publishers, 1998), p. 155.

be made not only to the drafting history of Article 14 of the CRC, but also to that of Article 18 of the CCPR. Since the text of Article 18 of the CCPR has been influenced amongst others by the Declaration on the Elimination of All Forms of Intolerance and of Discrimination based on Religion or Belief, adopted by the General Assembly of the United Nations in 1981,[2] this text will be taken into account in the interpretation of Article 18 of the CCPR[3] and hence indirectly also in that of Article 14 of the CRC. Moreover, general comments and views on individual complaints by the Human Rights Committee relating to Article 18(1) and (3) of the CCPR may serve to guide the interpretation of Article 14(1) and (3) of the CRC.

3. Similar use will be made of the activities of regional bodies, in particular the European Court of Human Rights. Yet the proviso needs to be made that interpretations that are made about a sensitive and contested issue such as religious freedom in the context of a regional mechanism may have limited relevance in a universal setting, where the diversity of religious convictions and of conceptions of State-Church relations is many times stronger.

4. To the extent that there are textual differences between Article 18 of the CCPR and Article 14 of the CRC, the drafting history of the CRC will be the first reference point to indicate whether or not a different substance was intended. In the second place, the practice of the Committee on the Rights of the Child will be looked at.

5. The most difficult issues however are those in which a child's freedom of thought, conscience and religion is opposed to the rights or interests of his or her parents or legal guardians. These situations will be examined under Article 14(2). In this field, neither the CCPR nor other non-child-specific texts can offer relevant guidance.

---

[2] GA Res. 36/55 of 25 November 1981.
[3] See M. Nowak, *U.N. Covenant on Civil and Political Rights, CCPR Commentary* (Kehl/Strasbourg/Arlington, N.P. Engel Publisher, 1993), p. 311.

CHAPTER TWO

COMPARISON WITH RELATED INTERNATIONAL
HUMAN RIGHTS PROVISIONS

1. Freedom of Thought, Conscience and Religion (Article 14(1) and (3))

6. The Universal Declaration of Human Rights (Article 18) and the International Covenant on Civil and Political Rights (Article 18) enounce the right to freedom of thought, conscience and religion at the universal level for 'everyone'. In addition, on the universal level the International Convention on the Elimination of All Forms of Racial Discrimination (Article 5) offers protection against racial discrimination in the enjoyment of this right, and the International Convention on the protection of the rights of all migrant workers and their families (Article 12) confirms this right for migrant workers and members of their families. The Member States of the Council of Europe are bound by Article 9 of the European Convention on human rights. The same right is moreover included in Article 10 of the Charter of Fundamental Rights of the European Union. The American Convention on Human Rights likewise protects freedom of conscience and religion for everyone within the jurisdiction of the OAS Member States (Article 12). In the African Charter on Human and Peoples' Rights (Article 8), the formulation is 'freedom of conscience, the profession and free practice of religion'. The African Charter on the Rights and Welfare of the Child likewise contains a provision on freedom of thought, conscience and religion (Article 9).

7. The formulation in the CRC differs from most of those other provisions (except Article 5 CERD) in that it is written from the perspective of the duty of the States Parties. This may result in a restriction of the scope of State obligations, since only the obligation to 'respect' the right is mentioned, which may exclude obligations to 'protect' and 'fulfil' (*cf. infra*, No. 22–23).

8. Most provisions group the freedoms of 'thought, conscience and religion'. Only in the American Convention and in the African Charter, the freedom of thought is omitted. In the American Convention, freedom of thought is protected in Article 13, together with freedom of expression.

9. Most provisions (except Article 9 CERD and the African texts) are significantly more detailed in their definition of the scope of the freedom of religion. They mention the freedom to have and adopt a religion of one's choice (Article 18 CCPR, Article 12 CMW) or the freedom to change one's religion or belief (Article 18 UDHR, Article 9 ECHR, Article 10 CFREU, Article 12 ACHR), as well as the freedom to manifest one's religion or belief, specifying certain modalities thereof (Article 18 UDHR, Article 18 CCPR, Article 12 CMW, Article 9 ECHR, Article 10 CFREU, Article 12 ACHR). In addition, Article 18 of the CCPR and Article 12 of the CMW protect against coercion impairing free choice in religion. Article 12 of the ACHR contains a similar provision, protecting against 'restrictions that might impair his freedom to maintain or to change his religion or beliefs'. Moreover this article is the only one to explicitly mention the freedom to 'disseminate' one's religion. Article 10(2) of the EU Charter of Fundamental Rights is the only one to recognize the right to conscientious objection. The formulation in Article 8 of the African Charter seems more restrictive than the other provisions, since freedom of religion is limited to 'the profession and free practice of religion'. This may exclude the right to choose a religion or the right to change religion. To what extent the absence of detail in Article 14 of the CRC compared to other provisions on the same right affects its substance, will be examined below.

10. In those provisions that include a specific limitation clause (Article 18 CCPR, Article 12 CMW, Article 9 ECHR, Article 12 ACHR), justifiable restrictions can only concern the freedom to manifest one's religion. Hence, the other aspects of the freedom of religion, as well as the freedoms of thought (except in the ACHR) and conscience, are absolute. The UDHR (Article 29(2)) and the CFREU (Article 52) have general limitation clauses, applicable to all aspects of the protected rights. The uniformity in the specific limitation clauses is striking: restrictions are justified when they are provided by law and necessary for the protection of public safety, (public) order, health, morals or the (fundamental) rights and freedoms of others. Article 8 of the ACHPR contains only a brief reference to law and order. In the African Charter on the Rights and Welfare of the Child, there is no mention of possible restrictions of the child's freedom of thought, conscience and religion, except in relation to the duties of parents in this respect. Hence, it seems that in the context of that Convention, children's freedom of thought, conscience and religion can be restricted by their parents, and that the State may sometimes interfere in the parents' exercise of their duties in this respect. Yet other types of direct State interference are prohibited.

11. Only in the CCPR (Article 4(2)), the freedom of thought, conscience and religion enjoys additional protection as a non-derogable right in time of public emergency.

2. Parental Guidance (Article 14(2))

12. A provision with the exact same content as Article 14(2) of the CRC is not found in any other convention. Article 9(2–3) of the African Charter on the Rights and Welfare of the Child comes closest, yet it mentions only a parental duty, not a right. However, since this is a duty that must be respected by the State, it appears to be the equivalent of a right.

13. The other provisions quoted below concern a distinct right, i.e. the right of parents or legal guardians to ensure the religious education of their children. Whereas the parental right in Article 14(2) is accessory to a right of the child (it is a right to guide the child in the exercise of his or her right), this other right is a proper right of the adults, of which the child is a passive object (undergoing the exercise of the parental rights).

14. On the universal level, such provisions are found in identical terms in the CCPR (Article 18(3), the CESCR (Article 13(3)) and the CMW (Article 12(4)). Moreover, Article 26(3) of the UDHR contains a very general provision, without specific reference to the religious aspect of education. Article 5(1)(b) of the UNESCO Convention against Discrimination in Education[4] contains one that is a little more elaborate, in that it refers to procedures in domestic law and that it adds that no one should be compelled to receive religious instruction inconsistent with his or her own conviction. This phrase not only offers protection against State indoctrination, but can equally serve as a basis for protecting children's rights against religious instruction imposed by their parents. On the regional level, the parents' right to choose their children's education in conformity with their religion is protected in Article 2 of the First Additional Protocol to the ECHR, Article 14(3) of the CFREU, Article 12(4) of the ACHR, and Article 11(4) of the ACRWC.

---

[4] Adopted on 14 December 1960 by the General Conference of UNESCO, entered into force on 22 May 1962.

CHAPTER THREE

SCOPE OF ARTICLE 14

1. *Introduction*

15. The CRC Committee's Guidelines for Periodic Reports require information on how the freedom of thought, conscience and religion, among other civil rights and freedoms, is 'recognized by law specifically in relation to children'.[5] The Committee has regularly expressed its concern that States give inadequate attention to the promotion of the civil rights and freedoms of the child, including freedom of thought, conscience and religion. Specific recognition of the child's freedom of religion in domestic legislation appears to be rare in practice.[6]

16. Reluctance to accept an autonomous right of the child in this field is also expressed in the large number of reservations and interpretative declarations that have been made with regard to Article 14. Several of those refer in rather general terms to national legislation, traditions or Islamic law.[7] Others offer more specific reasons, such as the existence of a State religion,[8] the fact that free choice in religion runs counter to Islamic Shari'a,[9] or the wish to safeguard the rights of parents in this sphere.[10]

17. Several other provisions of the CRC present a link with the freedom of thought, conscience and religion as protected in Article 14. Article 2 prohibits discrimination, amongst others on the basis of the religion of the

---

[5] CRC Committee, *General Guidelines regarding the form and the contents of the periodic reports* (UN Doc. CRC/C/58, 1996), para. 48.

[6] R. Hodgkin and P. Newell, *Implementation Handbook for the Convention on the Rights of the Child* (New York, UNICEF, 2002), p. 193.

[7] For example the reservations of Brunei Darussalam, Indonesia, Kiribati, Malaysia, Poland, Singapore, the Syrian Arab Republic and the United Arab Emirates. Several States issued objections against this type of reservations, claiming amongst others that they are indeterminate and overbroad.

[8] *Cf.* the reservations of Algeria, Morocco and the Maldives.

[9] *Cf.* the reservations of Iraq and Jordan.

[10] *Cf.* the reservation of the Holy See.

child or his or her parents or legal guardians. Article 8 protects the child's right to preserve his or her identity, which may include religious identity. Article 13 protects freedom of expression, which extends to expression in the religious sphere.[11] Similarly, the freedoms of association and of peaceful assembly (Article 15) include applications in the context of religion. Moreover, the child's right of access to information (Article 17) applies to information about religious matters.

18. The child's privacy right may also be related to his or her freedom of religion, for example when the mention of one's religious affiliation is mandatory in an official document. The Committee objected in this respect to the requirement in Greece that a student's secondary school graduation certificate indicate, where this is the case, that the student does not practise the Greek Orthodox religion. It noted that States should 'ensure that a child's religious affiliation, or lack of one, in no way hinders the child's rights, including the right to non-discrimination and to privacy, for example in the context of information included in the school graduation certificate.'[12]

19. Explicit protection of the child's religious freedom is included in Article 20(3), providing that alternative care arrangements must pay due regard to the child's religious background. Also, Article 30 protects the right of children belonging to religious minorities to profess and practice their own religion. For example, the Committee's deep concern in connection with State intervention in religion in Tibet was expressed under Article 30, rather than Article 14.[13]

20. Since children's introduction to religion is part of the educational process, a clear link can be established with Articles 28 and 29 on the right of the child to education. In particular, Article 29(1)(a) stipulates that the education of the child shall be directed to the preparation of the child for responsible life in a free society, in the spirit of understanding, peace, tolerance, equality of sexes, and friendship among all religious groups. In this respect,

---

[11] This was mentioned in the *Travaux Préparatoires*, in particular in the Considerations of the 1989 Working Group (UN Doc. E/CN.4/1989/48, para. 284), see S. Detrick (ed.), *The United Nations Convention on the Rights of the Child, A Guide to the "Travaux Préparatoires"* (Dordrecht/Boston/London, Martinus Nijhoff Publishers, 1992), p. 247.

[12] CRC Committee, *Concluding Observations: Greece* (UN Doc. CRC/C/15/Add.170, 2002), paras. 44–45.

[13] CRC Committee, *Concluding Observations: China* (UN Doc. CRC/C/15/Add.56, 1996), para. 20.

the Committee noted that laws banning schoolteachers from wearing head-scarves in public schools do 'not contribute to the child's understanding of the right to freedom of religion and to the development of an attitude of tolerance as promoted in the aims of education under Article 29 of the Convention'.[14] Moreover, issues with regard to religious instruction in schools can be brought both under Article 14 and Article 29.[15] Finally, the reference to international humanitarian law in Article 38 has some relevance for the protection of religious freedom, since international humanitarian law includes some provisions in this respect, amongst others with regard to the religious freedom of prisoners of war, civilian internees, protected persons and the population of occupied territories.

21. In its examination of State reports, the Committee does not focus solely on child-specific issues relating to freedom of thought, conscience and religion. Rather, it emphasizes that 'the human rights of children cannot be realized independently from the human rights of their parents, or in isolation from society at large'.[16] In that respect, it has recommended the enactment of protective legislation and the rescinding of legislation that is overly restrictive of religious freedom in general.[17] In this context, the Committee sometimes makes reference to other binding and non-binding human rights provisions relating to religious freedom,[18] as well as findings of other United Nations bodies.[19]

---

[14] CRC Committee, *Concluding Observations: Germany* (UN Doc. CRC/C/15/Add.226, 2004), para. 30.

[15] *E.g.* CRC Committee, *Concluding Observations: Italy* (UN Doc. CRC/C/15/Add.198, 2003), paras. 29–30.

[16] CRC Committee, *Concluding Observations: Uzbekistan* (UN Doc. CRC/C/15/Add.167, 2001), para. 6; CRC Committee, *Concluding Observations: Saudi Arabia* (UN Doc. CRC/C/15/Add. 148, 2001), para. 31; CRC Committee, *Concluding Observations: Iran* (CRC/C/15/Add.123, 2000), para. 35.

[17] CRC Committee, *Concluding Observations: Uzbekistan, o.c.* (note 16), paras. 6–7; CRC Committee, *Concluding Observations: Saudi Arabia, o.c.* (note 16), paras. 31–32; CRC Committee, *Concluding Observations*: Iran, *o.c.* (note 16), paras. 35–36.

[18] For example in CRC Committee, *Concluding Observations: Iran, o.c.* (note 16), paras. 35–36, the Committee mentions the 1981 Declaration on the Elimination of All Forms of Intolerance and of Discrimination Based on Religion or Belief, and Commission on Human Rights resolution 2000/33.

[19] For example in CRC Committee, *Concluding Observations: Iran, o.c.* (note 16), paras. 35–36, the Committee mentions the Human Rights Committee's General Comment No. 22 as well as findings of the Human Rights Committee and of the Committee on Economic, Social and Cultural Rights and recommendations made by the Special Rapporteur on the question of religious intolerance following his visit to the State Party.

> *2. Para. 1: 'States Parties shall respect the right of the child to freedom of thought, conscience and religion.'*

22. Does the phrase 'shall respect' refer only to negative State obligations, i.e. obligations not to actively interfere with the right, excluding the positive obligations to offer protection against interferences by third persons, and to actively fulfil the right? This is a difficult question to answer. The term 'respect' itself is ambiguous. On the one hand, the distinction between obligations to respect, protect and fulfil is gaining ground in international human rights law, and in that view, the obligation to respect is limited to negative State obligations. Yet on the other hand, this terminology is not yet generally used. For example the European Court of Human Rights does not apply it, and to the contrary gives a broader meaning to the term 'respect'. In particular, in the context of Article 9 of the ECHR, it was stated that 'there may also be positive obligations inherent in an effective 'respect' for the individual's freedom of religion.'[20]

23. At the time of the drafting of the CRC, the above-mentioned terminology was even less generally used. The drafting history nevertheless suggests a link between the choice of the term 'respect' and the unwillingness of some States to commit to far-reaching positive obligations, in particular obligations to fulfil. Other proposals included the expressions 'shall recognize' or 'shall ensure'. The words 'shall respect' were accepted as a solution after a division had arisen among the proponents of both other options. Apparently the reluctance to accept the term 'ensure' was related to a concern with the separation of Church and State, which indicates that some States read this term as implying active State involvement to protect religious freedom, which they rejected.[21] The *'travaux préparatoires'* thus indicate that the term 'respect' was not meant to include positive State obligations to fulfil this freedom. Yet since the concept of positive State obligations to protect the freedom against interventions by third persons (indirect horizontal effect) was not debated, the *travaux préparatoires* do not offer sufficient basis for a narrow interpretation of the term 'respect' that would exclude all such obligations.

24. The CRC Committee seems to have taken the viewpoint that States have a positive obligation under Article 14 to adopt legislation and take mea-

---

[20] ECmHR, No. 8160/78, *X v. United Kingdom*, 12 March 1981, D.R. 22, para. 3.
[21] S. Detrick (ed.), *o.c.* (note 11), p. 242.

sures to protect the right. In the Guidelines for Periodic Reports it requests States to 'indicate the measures adopted to ensure the child's freedom to manifest his or her religion or beliefs, including with regard to minorities or indigenous groups. Information should also be provided on measures to ensure respect for the child's rights in relation to any religious teaching in public schools or institutions.[22] Hence, the Committee in this manner reintroduces both the term and substance of the obligation 'to ensure'.

2.1   *Freedom of Thought*

25. The freedom of thought never played an important part as an independent right. On the one hand it has a broad scope, since 'thought' may relate to any subject, without requiring the link to an ethical conviction that is inherent in the term 'conscience'.[23]

26. On the other hand, the array of restrictions of the freedom of thought is rather limited, since the exercise of this right remains within a person's mind. When a thought is expressed, freedom of expression is at stake. Most interferences with the freedom of thought, for example the obligation to reveal one's thoughts, will simultaneously interfere with the right to protection of one's private life.[24]

27. However the protection of freedom of thought is significantly stronger than that of the right to protection of private life or the freedom of expression, since it is an absolute right, protected unconditionally. Since the restriction clause of para. 3 does not apply to freedom of thought, the authorities may never limit this right. This implies that they cannot compel a child to reveal his or her thoughts.[25]

28. The second paragraph of Article 14 does apply to freedom of thought: parents and legal guardians have both a right and a duty to provide direction to the child in the exercise of his or her freedom of thought, in a manner consistent with the evolving capacities of the child (*cf. infra*, No. 52 *et seq.*).

---

[22] CRC Committee, *General Guidelines regarding the form and the contents of the periodic reports* (UN Doc. CRC/C/58, 1996), para. 57.

[23] C. D. de Jong, *The Freedom of Thought, Conscience and Religion or Belief in the United Nations (1946–1992)* (Antwerpen/Groningen/Oxford, Intersentia/Hart, 2000), p. 22.

[24] *Cf.* in relation to Article 18 of the CCPR: Human Rights Committee, *General Comment No. 22: The right to freedom of thought, conscience and religion (Article 18)* (UN Doc. CCPR/C/21/Rev.1/Add.4, 1993), para. 3.

[25] The same applies to adults on the basis of Article 18 of the CCPR: Human Rights Committee, *General Comment No. 22, o.c.* (note 24), para. 3.

2.2   *Freedom of Conscience*

29. The scope of freedom of conscience is narrower than that of freedom of thought, since it is restricted to convictions of an ethical or philosophical nature. It is distinct from freedom of religion, since it does not require a metaphysical or supernatural element. One author aptly summarizes doctrinal opinion on this issue: 'There seems to be a consensus among the authors that this freedom refers to the right to have one's own convictions, which determine to a large extent one's way of living. No connection to a divine entity is necessary: just a strong ethical or philosophical belief may suffice, as long as it has a major impact on how to run one's life. All convictions will not be equally important in this respect: of the criteria mentioned, reference can be made to the genuineness of the conviction, the framework this conviction offers for Man's way of living and a certain amount of consistency and continuity. Lifelong consistency is not required, however, and the conviction does not have to be 'true' in an objective sense, as long as it is true for the person concerned. Nor does the conviction have to stem from an existing religion or belief; what counts is its subjective value.'[26] Issues such as pacifism,[27] vegetarianism[28] and environmental issues[29] have been treated as falling under the freedom of conscience.

30. The child's freedom of conscience may not be restricted by public authorities, since the restriction clause of para. 3 does not apply. Yet para. 2, concerning parental guidance in the exercise of this right, is applicable.

31. Does the State's duty to respect children's freedom of conscience prohibit States to impose on them a certain behaviour that would go against their convictions? According to de Jong, most authors emphasize this as an important aspect of the freedom of conscience.[30] Nowak, writing on Article 18 of the CCPR, is of the opposite opinion. In his interpretation, 'the freedom to live and act in harmony with one's conscience enjoys the absolute protection of (private) freedom of conscience so long as these actions do not affect the rights and freedoms of others. Once they leave this sphere of privacy, as in the case of the refusal to perform legal duties (*e.g.,* duty to pay taxes or serve in the military), they are protected by Article 18 only

---

[26] C.D. de Jong, *o.c.* (note 23), p. 21.
[27] *E.g.* ECmHR, No. 7050/75, *Arrowsmith* v. *United Kingdom*, 12 October 1978, *D.R.* 19, p. 5.
[28] R. Hodgkin and P. Newell, *o.c.* (note 6), p. 195.
[29] *Ibid.*
[30] C.D. de Jong, *o.c.* (note 23), p. 22.

when they represent a practice or some other form of public manifestation of a religion or belief.'[31] If the first-mentioned interpretation is to be followed, State obligations are far-reaching, in the light of the absolute nature of this freedom. When the State imposes behaviour going against *religious* convictions, requests for exemptions are generally treated under the right to manifest one's religion by observing its rules and practices. Yet that right is subject to legitimate restrictions. For example, the European Commission of Human Rights held that a State was allowed to oblige a child belonging to the Seventh Day Adventists to attend Saturday School, since this was justified for the protection of the child's right to education.[32]

32. If the scope of Article 14 is limited to negative State obligations (*cf. supra* No. 22–23), there seem to be only two options: either Article 14 does not encompass a State obligation to refrain from imposing behaviour going against an individual's conscience. In that event, the protection of the freedom of conscience is restricted to the inner forum, excluding the freedom to live according to one's conscience, and States do not have to take conscientious objections into account the same way they might take into account religious objections. Or, alternatively, Article 14 does include such a State obligation, which then necessarily is absolute, meaning that States have no power whatsoever to impose behaviour going against individual conscience, regardless of the considerations of general interest they might be able to invoke.

33. Yet if it is accepted that Article 14 includes positive State obligations, a middle road can be taken, by analysing claims for exemptions from general rules in the light of positive State obligations.[33] The positive obligations of the State to protect and fulfil freedom of conscience may create a duty for the State to make arrangements for exemptions from general rules in cases where such rules conflict with certain individuals' conscience. The scope of positive State obligations is not unlimited, and in evaluating whether such obligations have been violated, general interest considerations are normally taken into account. This approach would thus lead to a balancing exercise between the freedom of conscience on the one hand and general interests underlying the State's rule or policy on the other, such that in

---

[31] M. Nowak, *o.c.* (note 3), p. 315.
[32] ECmHR, No. 44888/98, *Martins Casimiro and Cerveira Ferreira* v. *Luxemburg*, 27 April 1999, not reported.
[33] *E.g.* (in a case concerning an adult) ECmHR, No. 8160/78, *o.c.* (note 20), para. 3.

some situations, but not in other, the State would be prevented from imposing behaviour going against an individual's conscience.

34. One of the issues for which this debate is relevant, is conscientious objection to military service, when it is not based on religion, but rather on other convictions such as pacifism. The Optional Protocol on the involvement of children in armed conflict requires States Parties to ensure that persons who have not attained the age of 18 years are not compulsorily recruited into their armed forces (Article 2). Yet for those States who have not yet ratified this protocol, the rule remains that of Article 38 of the CRC, which prohibits recruitment into the armed forces only under the age of 15, and conscientious objection remains an issue for 15- to 18-year-olds. In its General Comment No. 22 on Article 18 of the CCPR, the Human Rights Committee stated that it believes that a right to conscientious objection can be derived from Article 18, 'inasmuch as the obligation to use lethal force may seriously conflict with the freedom of conscience and the right to manifest one's religion or belief'.[34] The Committee thus bases this right also on the freedom of conscience. At the same time the Committee seems to limit it to a right to refuse to use lethal force, and does not add the conclusion that all States are required to exempt conscientious objectors from military service or the use of lethal force. Hence the Committee's viewpoint on this matter remains ambiguous.

35. When conscientious objection is not based on religion, the answer to the question whether States are obliged to provide exemptions for conscientious objectors depends on the answers to the question whether this is to be treated as an issue of negative or positive State obligations (*cf. supra*, No. 33). If the State's obligation is a negative one, the answer depends on the scope of freedom of conscience. If it is a merely private right, as Nowak sees it (*cf. supra*, No. 31), there is no protection for such conscientious objectors. Yet in the other interpretation, this protection is absolute. If on the other hand the State's obligation is a positive one, the answer depends on a balancing between the freedom of conscience on the one hand, and general interests (such as national security) invoked by the State on the other, which will determine the scope of the State's positive obligation. In that respect, the situation is comparable to that of conscientious objection based on religion, when similar balancing will be required under article 14(3), to determine whether or not State interference with the freedom to manifest

---

[34] Human Rights Committee, *General Comment No. 22, o.c.* (note 24), para. 11.

one's religion or belief is justified. The present state of international law offers some support for interpreting the freedom of conscience and religion in such a way that it includes a right to conscientious objection, at least to the use of lethal force, yet does not allow to conclude that it is mandatory for States to recognize and respect such a right. A 1987 resolution of the Commission on Human Rights[35] appeals to States to recognize conscientious objection to military service as a legitimate exercise of the freedom of thought, conscience and religion, and invites States to exempt conscientious objectors from military service, yet without defining this as a right. This was reiterated several times since then.[36] Then there was the above-quoted somewhat ambiguous statement in the 1993 General Comment No. 22 of the Human Rights Committee (*cf. supra*, No. 34).

36. In 1999, the Human Rights Committee examined an individual complaint of a person whose application for recognition as a conscientious objector had been rejected because the type of (non-religious) objections he advanced, did not fall within the criteria of Dutch law, which required 'an unsurmountable objection of conscience to military service . . . because of the use of violent means'.[37] In its views, the Human Rights Committee referred to the statement in its General Comment No. 22 that the right to conscientious objection to military service can be derived from Article 18. Yet in its view, Dutch legislation, providing for exemptions for conscientious objectors, was compatible with Article 18 of the CCPR. It saw no reason to doubt the national authorities' finding that this case fell outside the scope of this provision and hence there was no interference with the applicant's freedom of conscience. From this case may be drawn several conclusions with regard to the Human Rights Committee's interpretation of the freedom of conscience in Article 18 of the CCPR. In the first place, the freedom of conscience is no longer seen as a purely private freedom. Otherwise, the Human Rights Committee would not even examine whether the imposition of sanctions to enforce the performance of military duty constitutes an infringement of

---

[35] Resolution 1987/46, UN Doc. E/CN.4/1987/60.
[36] Resolution 1989/59, UN Doc. E/1989/20, 139–142. This text 'recognizes' the right to have conscientious objections to military service as a legitimate exercise of the right to freedom of thought, conscience and religion, and 'appeals' to States to provide for exemptions. Later resolutions (Resolution 1993/84; Resolution 1995/83, UN Doc. E/CN.4.1995/176; Resolution 1998/77) 'draw attention to' this right, and continue to appeal to States to provide for exemptions.
[37] Human Rights Committee, No. 682/1996, *Paul Westerman* v. *The Netherlands*, views of 3 November 1999.

his right to freedom of conscience. In the second place, it is not clear on the basis of this case alone, whether the limits of the right to freedom of conscience are determined only by the type of convictions that fall within the scope of this freedom (the freedom being absolute, because it concerns negative State obligations falling outside the scope of the restriction clause), or whether in addition they are also determined by a balancing exercise with other interests (the freedom not being absolute, because it concerns positive State obligations). The Human Rights Committee's statement that 'the right to freedom of conscience does not as such imply the right to refuse all obligations imposed by law, nor does it provide immunity from criminal liability in respect of every refusal' (para. 9.3.) can be interpreted in either way. Yet the first hypothesis can be excluded, when these views are read in combination with the Human Rights Committee's decisions in two cases concerning conscientious objection to the payment of the percentage of taxes that is to be spent on military expenditures.[38] In those cases, the Human Rights Committee stated that 'although Article 18 of the Covenant certainly protects the right to manifest one's conscience by opposing military activities and expenditures, the refusal to pay taxes on the grounds of conscientious objection clearly falls outside the scope of protection of this article'.[39] Before the Human Rights Committee's General Comment No. 22 in 1993 and its views in the Westerman case in 1999, this could be interpreted in the sense that 'manifestations' of freedom of conscience were protected only as long as they remained within the private sphere. Yet this is not compatible with the more far-reaching recognition given in those later texts to the right to conscientious objection to military service. That interpretation being excluded, those cases clearly show that the limits of the freedom of conscience are not based solely on the type of convictions falling within its scope. In those cases, the Human Rights Committee indicated explicitly that the type of convictions do fall under freedom of conscience, yet there is no obligation on the State to recognize those convictions in the way requested by the applicants. Although the very succinct motivation of these decisions of inadmissibility does not reveal the

---

[38] Human Rights Committee, No. 446/1991, *Dr. J.P. v. Canada*, inadmissibility decision of 7 November 1991, and Human Rights Committee, No. 483/1991, *J.v.K. and C.M.G.v.K.-S. v. The Netherlands*, inadmissibility decision of 23 July 1992.

[39] Human Rights Committee, No. 446/1991, *o.c.* (note 38), para. 4.2. In the other case (para. 4.2) it was phrased slightly differently: 'Although Article 18 of the Covenant certainly protects the right to hold, express and disseminate opinions and convictions, including conscientious objection to military. . . .'

underlying reasoning of the Human Rights Committee, this seems compatible with a reasoning based on the limits of positive State obligations.

37. While the Westerman case thus supports the conclusion that a State forcing conscientious objectors to take part in armed combat would violate Article 18 of the CCPR, the scope of the State's obligation to respect conscientious objections to military violence remains unclear. For example can such individuals be forced to bear arms during training, or can they be forced to perform unarmed military service? When an alternative to military service exists, the Human Rights Committee examines under Article 26 of the ICCPR whether or not it is discriminatory, for example because of its length or punitive character.[40]

38. On condition that the existence of positive State obligations under Article 14(1) of the CRC is accepted (*cf. supra*, No. 22–23), the above-described reasoning of the Human Rights Committee under Article 18 of the CCPR can be applied also to Article 14 of the CRC.

39. The Inter-American Commission on Human Rights has not yet examined any individual complaints relating to conscientious objection. Yet in its 1997 annual report, it noted: 'The Commission also invites the member States whose legislation still does not exempt conscientious objectors from military service or alternative service, to review their legal regimes and make modifications consistent with the spirit of the international law of human rights.'[41] On the one hand, the reference to 'the international law of human rights' brings in the ambiguity described above. On the other hand, the Inter-American Commission clearly interprets the international law of human rights in such a way that it imposes a duty to provide exemptions from military service for conscientious objections and, it seems, even exemptions from alternative service.

40. The European Commission and Court of Human Rights have never recognized a right for conscientious objectors to be exempted from any type of military service.[42] Yet the Parliamentary Assembly of the Council of Europe

---

[40] Human Rights Committee, No. 295/1988, *Aapo Jarvinen v. Finland*, views of 25 July 1990.
[41] Annual Report of the Inter-American Commission on Human Rights, 1997, OE/Ser.L/V/II.98 doc.6 rev., chap. VII, 10°.
[42] The European Commission on Human Rights dismissed several complaints as inadmissible. See D.J. Harris, M. O'Boyle and C. Warbrick, *Law of the European Convention on Human Rights* (London, Butterworths, 1996), pp. 368–369. A case before the European Court of Human Rights ended in a friendly settlement: ECtHR, *Dimitrov and others v. Bulgaria*, 10 April 2001, not reported.

has been promoting a right to exemption from armed service for reasons of conscience since 1967, recommending amongst others the introduction of such right into the European Convention on Human Rights.[43] Moreover, the Committee of Ministers of the Council of Europe recommended the provision of legal exemptions from compulsory military service for conscientious objectors in all Member States.[44] The Charter of Fundamental Rights of the European Union (*cf. supra*) explicitly recognizes the right to conscientious objection. Yet this text is not binding as such. Moreover, its scope is defined with reference to national law.

2.3   Freedom of Religion

41. Most other international provisions on freedom of religion (*cf. supra*) include some detail about the scope of this freedom. In particular, Article 18(1) of the CCPR states: 'This right shall include the freedom to have or to adopt a religion or belief of his choice, and freedom, either individually or in community with others, and in public or private, to manifest his religion or belief in worship, observance, practice and teaching.' The only detail found in this respect in the CRC, is in the third paragraph of Article 14, which mentions the 'freedom to manifest one's religion or beliefs'. Hence, it is clear that the freedom of religion is not intended as a purely internal freedom. What is not clear however, is what types of manifestations are included, nor whether the right to change one's religion is protected under Article 14.

42. During the drafting of Article 14, a paragraph including language similar to that of Article 18(1) of the CCPR was adopted by the Working Group at first reading,[45] but eventually it appeared not possible to reach a con-

---

[43] Parliamentary Assembly resolution 337 (1967) on the right of conscientious objection, recommendation 816 (1977) on the right of conscientious objection to military service, and recommendation 1518 (2001) on the exercise of the right of conscientious objection to military service in Council of Europe member States.

[44] Committee of Ministers of the Council of Europe, Recommendation No. R (87) 8, adopted on 9 April 1987.

[45] The proposed paragraph 2 read: 'This right shall include in particular the freedom to have or to adopt a religion or whatsoever belief of his choice and freedom, either individually or in community with others and in public or private, to manifest his religion or belief, subject only to such limitations as are prescribed by law and are necessary to protect public safety, order, health and morals; and the right to have access to education in the matter of religion or belief.' S. Detrick, *o.c.* (note 11), p. 246.

sensus on it. The controversy related not to the details of the manifestation of religion, but rather to the freedom of the child to choose and change his or her religion or belief.[46] The debate about the right to change one's religion exists also within the context of Article 18 of the CCPR. Concerning the right to choose one's religion, the controversy seems to have been focused on the existence of a child's own right, *vis-à-vis* his or her parents, rather than on the protection of the choice in religion *vis-à-vis* public authorities. Hence apart from these problematic issues, there is no objection to an interpretation of the scope of the freedom of religion in Article 14(1) of the CRC in line with that in Article 18(1) of the CCPR.

43. The recognition of a State religion or of several official religions does not in itself violate religious freedom.[47] Yet both the Human Rights Committee[48] and the Committee on the Rights of the Child[49] have warned that there is a risk that this may give rise to discrimination.

44. Since the limitation clause of Article 14(3) applies only to the freedom to manifest one's religion or beliefs, the aspects of the freedom of religion that do not concern the manifestation of religion, are absolute freedoms. These include the right to have or not to have a religion, as well as the protection of free choice of religion *vis-à-vis* public authorities. These elements are essential to the concept of freedom of religion. The negative freedom of religion (i.e. the freedom not to have a religion of belief) is stressed explicitly in the Human Rights Committee's General Comment No. 22 on Article 18 of the CCPR,[50] as well as in the case law of the European Court of Human Rights.[51] If the freedom to change one's religion is included (*cf. infra*, No. 49), it is likewise an absolute freedom (at least in the relationship between the child and the State). Moreover, some aspects of the practice of religion, which have a strictly private character, fall outside the concept of

---

[46] S. Detrick, *o.c.* (note 11), p. 247.
[47] *Cf.* Human Rights Committee, *General Comment No. 22, o.c.* (note 24), para. 9.
[48] *Ibid.*
[49] CRC Committee, *Concluding Observations: Indonesia* (UN Doc. CRC/C/15/Add.7, 1993), para. 15 and CRC Committee, *Concluding Observations: Indonesia* (CRC/C/15/Add.25, 1994), para. 13.
[50] Human Rights Committee, *General Comment No. 22, o.c.* (note 24), para. 2: 'Article 18 protects theistic, non-theistic and atheistic beliefs, as well as the right not to profess any religion or belief.'
[51] See for example ECtHR, *Buscarini and others* v. *San Marino*, 18 February 1999, *Reports of Judgments and Decisions*, 1999–I, para. 34: 'it is also a precious asset for atheists, agnostics, sceptics and the unconcerned. (. . .)That freedom entails, *inter alia*, freedom to hold or not to hold religious beliefs and to practise or not to practise a religion'.

'manifesting' one's religion, and must therefore have an absolute character. One may think in the first place of prayers and other religious rituals performed at home.[52]

45. In its General Comment No. 22 on Article 18 of the CCPR, the Human Rights Committee states: 'The terms 'belief' and 'religion' are to be broadly construed. Article 18 is not limited in its application to traditional religions or to religions and beliefs with institutional characteristics or practices analogous to those of traditional religions. The Committee therefore views with concern any tendency to discriminate against any religion or belief for any reason, including the fact that they are newly established, or represent religious minorities that may be the subject of hostility on the part of a predominant religious community'.[53] There is no reason to adopt a different interpretation of Article 14 of the CRC in this respect. This is particularly relevant for the debate that exists in several States about the issue of 'sects', and the protection of minors against them. Denying or severely restricting religious freedom solely on the basis of the qualification of a religious group as a sect is not compatible with either Article 18 of the CCPR or Article 14 of the CRC. A child or adult's right to join a small religious group that some may label a sect is protected to the same extent as a child or adult's right to join one of the major world religions. This matter is to be distinguished from that of the restriction of certain manifestations of a religion, which may be allowed for example because of their harmful effect on minors.

46. Despite the absence of detailed language, there is no reason to interpret the external aspect of religious freedom, i.e. the freedom to manifest religion or beliefs in Article 14 of the CRC differently from that in Article 18 of the CCPR. According to the text of Article 18(1) of the CCPR, the manifestation of religion or belief can be done either individually or in community with others, and in public or private, through worship, observance, practice and teaching. The Human Rights Committee interpreted this as follows in its General Comment No. 22 on Article 18: 'The concept of worship extends to ritual and ceremonial acts giving direct expression to belief, as well as various practices integral to such acts, including the building of places of worship, the use of ritual formulae and objects, the display of symbols, and the observance of holidays and days of rest. The observance and practice of religion or belief may include not only ceremonial acts but also

---

[52] *Cf.* M. Nowak, *o.c.* (note 3), p. 319.
[53] Human Rights Committee, *General Comment No. 22, o.c.* (note 24), para. 2.

such customs as the observance of dietary regulations, the wearing of distinctive clothing or head coverings,[54] participation in rituals associated with certain stages of life, and the use of a particular language customarily spoken by a group. In addition, the practice and teaching of religion or belief includes acts integral to the conduct by religious groups of their basic affairs, such as the freedom to choose their religious leaders, priests and teachers, the freedom to establish seminaries or religious schools and the freedom to prepare and distribute religious texts or publications.'.[55] Clearly, the manifestation of religion or beliefs sometimes involves the exercise of other rights protected in the CRC: the freedom to impart information and ideas either orally, in writing or in print, in the form of art or through any other media of the child's choice (Article 13), the freedom of (religious) association and the freedom of peaceful assembly (Article 15). The right to disseminate one's religion and to attempt to persuade others to convert to it (proselytism) is included in the protection of religious freedom according to the European Court of Human Rights: '(Article 9 of the ECHR) includes in principle the right to try to convince one's neighbour, for example through 'teaching', failing which, moreover, 'freedom to change [one's] religion or belief', enshrined in Article 9, would be likely to remain a dead letter.'[56] Moreover, the freedom to manifest one's religion must necessarily have as a counterpart the freedom not to manifest one's religion, an aspect bordering on the protection of one's privacy (Article 16 of the CRC).

47. Although this is a broad range of acts, it does not extend to all claims or activities based on religion. The definition of the Human Rights Committee is in principle compatible with the distinction made by the European Court of Human Rights between acts that 'actually express' or that are 'intimately linked to' religion or belief on the one hand, and acts that are simply motivated or influenced by a religion or belief, the latter category being excluded from the scope of Article 9 of the ECHR.[57] In a recent case, the European Court of Human Rights judged for example that the right to manifest one's religion did not include a right for pharmacists to refuse to sell contracep-

---

[54] This is confirmed by the CRC Committee with regard to the wearing of Muslim headscarves by girls in schools: CRC Committee, *Concluding Observations: Tunisia* (UN Doc. CRC/C/15/Add.181, 2002), para. 29.

[55] Human Rights Committee, *General Comment No. 22*, o.c. (note 24), para. 4.

[56] ECtHR, *Kokkinakis v. Greece*, 25 May 1993, *Publications of the Court*, Series A, 260-A, para. 31.

[57] See S. Stavros, 'Freedom of Religion and Claims for Exemption from Generally Applicable, Neutral Laws: Lessons from Across the Pond?', *European Human Rights Law Review*, 1997, pp. 616–617.

tives, even though this refusal may be based on their religion.[58] Yet when certain behaviour is not protected under the freedom to manifest one's religion, there may in some cases nevertheless exist a positive State obligation to provide for an exemption from a general rule in order to allow for this behaviour (cf. supra, No. 33). The fact that certain acts fall within the scope of Article 14 however does not mean that they cannot be restricted, since the restriction clause of Article 14(3) applies specifically to the manifestation of religion or beliefs (cf. infra, No. 65).

48. One of the most important child-specific aspects of religious freedom, is religious education. Article 5(2) of the Declaration on the Elimination of All Forms of Intolerance and of Discrimination Based on Religion or Belief states: 'Every child shall enjoy the right to have access to education in the matter of religion or belief in accordance with the wishes of his parents or, as the case may be, legal guardians, and shall not be compelled to receive teaching on religion or belief against the wishes of his parents or legal guardians, the best interests of the child being the guiding principle.' The exclusive focus in this provision on the wishes of parents and legal guardians, disregarding those of the child, is of course not compatible with Article 14 of the CRC (cf. infra, No. 52 et seq.). Yet the right itself must probably be considered as included, since without it, the child's freedom of religion is deprived of much of its significance. Moreover, the right of access to education was included in an early version of Article 14 of the CRC.[59] It was later abandoned in the context of the compromise that left out all details about the scope of the child's freedom of religion. Since there is no indication that the omission of this phrase was related to the wish to exclude the right of access to religious education, this earlier text can be interpreted as an indication that the drafters assumed it to be included. The right to religious education has both a positive and a negative aspect. The negative aspect protects against religious indoctrination by the State (for example the imposition of mandatory religious courses on all students regardless of their religion) and – if the positive State obligation to protect is recognized (cf. supra, No. 22–23) – by private actors other than the parents and legal guardians. The issue of protection against indoctrination by parents and legal guardians must be discussed in the context of the child's freedom of

[58] ECtHR, *Pichon and Sajous v. France*, decision of 2 October 2001, *Reports* 2001–X.
[59] Considerations 1983 Working Group (UN Doc. E/CN.4.1983/62, 1983), para. 57. The text read: 'The States parties shall ensure that (. . .) every child shall enjoy the right to have access to education in the matter of religion or belief in accordance with the wishes of his parents or, as the case may be, legal guardians (. . .)'. See S. Detrick, *o.c.* (note 11), p. 240.

choice in religious matters (*cf. infra*, No. 60). The positive aspect of the right to religious education certainly includes a negative State obligation to abstain from creating obstacles that would impede children's access to religious education. It may also include a positive obligation to offer protection against obstacles created by others (for example community leaders). Whether it includes protection against obstacles created by the parents or legal guardians, will be discussed under Article 14(2). That is also the appropriate heading to examine to what extent public authorities may interfere with the contents of religious education (for example in schools). Finally, there might in theory be a positive State obligation to provide religious education, for example by making room for this in the curriculum and providing the necessary funding. For example, Article 24(3.2) of the Belgian Constitution provides: 'All pupils of school age have the right to moral or religious education at the Community's expense'. Yet the drafting history of Article 14 of the CRC pleads against such an interpretation. In the context of the debate over the terms 'respect' or 'ensure', the US representative made it clear that she did not favour an interpretation that would oblige the State to provide religious education. This reasoning seems to have been followed by the drafters.[60]

49. Whether the freedom of religion includes the right to change one's religion is a contentious issue, in particular since under Islamic law, apostasy is a crime. Article 18 of the UDHR explicitly mentions the right to change one's religion, and this was one of the reasons for the abstention of Saudi Arabia during the General Assembly vote. At the drafting of the CCPR, there was not sufficient support for the inclusion of a similar provision in Article 18 of the CCPR. Yet the reference to the 'freedom to have or to adopt a religion or belief of his choice' can only be interpreted as including the right to change one's religion.[61] This was confirmed by the Human Rights Committee in its General Comment No. 22 on Article 18, stating that 'the freedom to 'have or to adopt' a religion or belief necessarily entails the freedom to choose a religion or belief, including the right to replace one's current religion or belief with another or to adopt atheistic views, as well as the right to retain one's religion or belief.'[62] Yet during the drafting of Article 14 of the CRC, there was no consensus on the inclusion of a similar phrase. Hence, it remains uncertain whether the child's freedom to change his or her religion is protected under this provision. Yet there seems to be a stronger

---

[60] S. Detrick, *o.c.* (note 11), p. 242.
[61] M. Nowak, *o.c.* (note 3), p. 316.
[62] Human Rights Committee, *General Comment No. 22, o.c.* (note 24), para. 5.

case in favour of an interpretation that includes this aspect than in favour of its opposite. In the first place, the ordinary meaning of 'freedom of religion' is hard to reconcile with a situation in which one would be compelled to adhere to a religion against one's own conscience. Secondly, it is not clear from the drafting history to what extent the opposition to the inclusion of the child's right to choose and change his or her religion is based specifically on the problem of apostasy, rather than on a reluctance to children's autonomy in this field, undermining parental rights. Thirdly, several Islamic States made reservations to Article 14 of the CRC indicating that they do not recognize the child's right to choose a different religion from Islam.[63] This indicates that in the eyes of these States, the text of Article 14 of the CRC as such may be interpreted as incorporating this right.

50. The same reasoning applies to the child's right to choose his or her religion, from the perspective of State-individual relations. When the child's choice in religion is seen in relation to parental choice, the second paragraph of Article 14 enters into play (*cf. infra*, No. 60).

51. The observance of religious rules or practices sometimes enters into conflict with legal rules. Hence legal issues concerning religious freedom are often framed in terms of granting or refusing a religious exemption from a general rule. For example, Muslim students who want to wear a headscarf in school, ask for an exemption from school rules prohibiting the wearing of headgear. A refusal to grant a religious exemption is to be examined under the limitation clause of Article 14(3) (*cf. infra*, No. 65 *et seq.*). Yet when the link with religious rules or practices is tenuous, the request for an exemption will be considered to fall outside the scope of Article 14.[64]

---

[63] See in particular the reservations of
— Iraq: 'The Government of Iraq has seen fit to accept (. . .) subject to a reservation in respect to article 14, paragraph 1, concerning the child's freedom of religion, as allowing a child to change his or her religion runs counter to the provisions of the Islamic Shariah.'
— Jordan: 'The Hashemite Kingdom of Jordan expresses its reservation and does not consider itself bound by articles 14 (. . .), which grant the child the right to freedom of choice of religion (. . .), since they are at variance with the precepts of the tolerant Islamic Shariah.'
— Oman: 'The Sultanate does not consider itself bound by those provisions of article 14 of the Convention that accord a child the right to choose his or her religion (. . .)'.
[64] *Cf.* under the CCPR, Human Rights Committee, No. 446/1991, *o.c.* (note 38): the refusal of a member of the Quakers to pay taxes that contribute to military activities and expenditures falls outside the scope of protection of Article 18 of the CCPR.

3. Para. 2: 'States Parties shall respect the rights and duties of the parents and, when applicable, legal guardians, to provide direction to the child in the exercise of his or her right in a manner consistent with the evolving capacities of the child.'

52. Article 14(2) reiterates Article 5 of the CRC: 'States Parties shall respect the responsibilities, rights and duties of parents or, where applicable, the members of the extended family or community as provided for by the local custom, legal guardians or other persons legally responsible for the child, to provide, in a manner consistent with the evolving capacities of the child, appropriate direction and guidance in the exercise by the child of the rights recognized in the present Convention.' The omission of 'responsibilities' and of the words 'appropriate' and 'guidance' does not affect the substance. Moreover, the omission of the reference to other caretakers except parents and legal guardians is not significant, since Article 5 applies also to the child's freedom of thought, conscience and religion. Hence direction in religious and philosophical matters can be a right or duty of members of the extended family or community or of other persons than parents or legal guardians who are legally responsible for the child. More remarkable is the omission of a paragraph similar to Article 18(4) of the CCPR and provisions in other general conventions (*cf. supra*, No. 13–14) concerning autonomous parental rights with regard to the religious and moral education of their children. The drafting history of Article 14 of the CRC shows that in the text adopted by the Working Group at first reading, a fourth paragraph was included, modelled on Article 18(4) of the CCPR, but different in the crucial respect of adding the child's choice on equal footing with that of the parents.[65] This paragraph was dropped in the final version, yet the present text goes even further in shifting the paradigm, because in Article 14(2) of the CRC the parental right is an accessory to the child's right, rather than an autonomous right on an equal footing.

53. This provision does not have a direct equivalent in any general human rights convention. On the one hand, it protects the parents' and legal guardians' educational role in religious and philosophical matters against State intervention. On the other hand, this provision guides the balancing between that educational role and the child's autonomous freedom of

---

[65] 'The States Parties shall equally respect the liberty of the child and his parents and, where applicable, legal guardians, to ensure the religious and moral education of the child in conformity with convictions of their choice.' S. Detrick, *o.c.* (note 11), p. 246.

thought, conscience and religion. Under general human rights conventions, the first role is covered by provisions such as Article 18(4) of the CCPR, protecting the liberty of parents and legal guardians to ensure the religious and moral education of their children in conformity with their own convictions. Conflicts between parents and children in this context then concern a conflict between that parental right and the child's freedom of thought, conscience and religion, as protected for example in Article 18(1) of the CCPR.

54. In the first place, Article 14(2) obliges the State to abstain from interfering with the religious and philosophical education that is offered by the parents. The limitation clause of Article 14(3) does not apply to the right of parents and legal guardians under Article 14(2). This right is limited only by the condition that it be exercised 'in a manner consistent with the evolving capacities of the child'. Hence, State interference cannot be justified by any general interest such as public order or the protection of morals, nor by a concern for the protection of the freedom of others. It can only be justified by the need to protect the child's freedom of religion. The parental guidance has to remain accessory to the child's right, and has to recede as the child's capacities evolve (*cf. infra*, No. 59).

55. The risk of the State usurping the parental guidance role is probably strongest in the context of public education. The drafting history of Article 14 (*cf. supra* No. 48) shows that States did not wish to commit themselves to a positive obligation to provide religious education in public schools. Yet when there is no room for religious instruction in the public school curriculum, the right to conduct religious education elsewhere must be ensured. In either case, State authorities should not interfere with the content of these teachings. Moreover, any kind of religious or moral education in the course of the mandatory school curriculum risks interfering with the right of parental guidance. Hence, some of the Human Rights Committee's statements on Article 18(4) of the CCPR, in General Comment No. 22 are relevant also in this context: 'Article 18.4 permits public school instruction in subjects such as the general history of religions and ethics if it is given in a neutral and objective way'[66] and 'public education that includes instruction

---

[66] See also Human Rights Committee, No. 40/1987, *Hartikainen v. Finland*, views of 9 April 1981. This is consistent with the approach of the European Court of Human Rights: ' (...) the second sentence of Article 2 of the Protocol (P1–2) does not prevent States from imparting through teaching or education information or knowledge of a directly or indirectly religious or philosophical kind. It does not even permit parents to object to the integration of

in a particular religion or belief is inconsistent with Article 18.4 unless provision is made for non-discriminatory exemptions or alternatives that would accommodate the wishes of parents and guardians'.[67] In the CRC context, in addition the wishes of the children should be taken into account. State-imposed religious or moral instruction interferes in the first place with the child's autonomous freedom of thought, conscience and religion protected in Article 14(1), and only in the second place with the right of parental guidance in the exercise of this right.

56. The CRC Committee is concerned not only with legal regulations, but also with practice. With regard to Myanmar for example, it noted with 'particular concern' the fact 'that children considered poor are channelled towards monastic Buddhist schools and are offered no alternative educational opportunity'.[68] With respect to Poland it noted its concern that 'despite regulations guaranteeing that parents can choose for their children to attend ethics classes instead of religion classes in public schools, in practice few schools offer ethics courses to allow for such a choice (...)' and recommended 'that the State Party ensure that all public schools permit children, in practice, to choose freely whether to attend religion or ethics classes (...)'[69] In its observations on a report of Italy, the Committee broadened State obligations by recommending 'that the State Party make sure that parents, in particular of foreign origin, when they are filling out the relevant forms, are aware that Catholic religious instruction is not compulsory'.[70] In the same context, the Committee expressed its concern that 'children, especially in elementary schools, may suffer from marginalization if they abstain from religious instruction, which is mainly covering Catholic religion'.[71] Yet it did not recommend any particular course of action

---

such teaching or education in the school curriculum, for otherwise all institutionalized teaching or education would run the risk of proving impracticable. (...) The second sentence of Article 2 (P1–2) implies on the other hand that the State, in fulfilling the functions assumed by it in regard to education and teaching, must take care that information or knowledge included in the curriculum is conveyed in an objective, critical and pluralistic manner. The State is forbidden to pursue an aim of indoctrination that might be considered as not respecting parents' religious and philosophical convictions. That is the limit that must not be exceeded.' (ECtHR, *Kjeldsen, Busk Madsen and Pedersen* v. *Denmark*, 7 December 1976, *Publications of the Court*, Series A, No. 23, para. 53.

[67] Human Rights Committee, *General Comment No. 22*, o.c. (note 24), para. 6.
[68] CRC Committee, *Concluding Observations: Myanmar* (UN Doc. CRC/C/15/Add.69, 1997), para. 16.
[69] CRC Committee, *Concluding Observations: Poland* (UN Doc. CRC/C/15/Add.194, 2002), paras. 32–33.
[70] CRC Committee, *Concluding Observations: Italy*, o.c. (note 15), para. 30.
[71] *Ibid.*, para. 29.

to deal with this issue. In its concluding observations on a report by Norway, the Committee showed concern with the process of exemption from the curriculum on 'Religions, Knowledge and Ethical Education'.[72] The Norwegian law introducing this new curriculum in 1998, provided that a pupil may be exempted from parts of the teaching if the parents apply in writing for such exemption on the grounds that these parts involve the practice of a religion or support for a particular philosophy of life. A pupil who has reached the age of 15 may himself or herself apply for exemption. Requests for exemptions from obviously religious activities would be granted automatically, yet in other cases, reasons must be stated, subject to privacy protection. From the concluding observations and summary record, it is however not clear in what respect the Committee considers this procedure to be inadequate. Since it mentions both children and parents, its concern is not merely with the autonomous right of children under 15. Probably it is the Committee's opinion that the exemption process should not require a statement of reasons.[73]

57. Offering direction to the child in the exercise of his or her right to freedom of thought, conscience and religion is also a duty for parents and legal guardians. In order to avoid duplicating the State obligation to respect the parental right in this matter, the State obligation to respect this parental duty can only mean that the State sometimes has to interfere in order to encourage or even oblige parents to fulfil their duty of guidance. This implies that the term 'respect' in this context cannot be limited to negative State obligations, as in the distinction between obligations to respect, protect and fulfil (cf. supra, No. 22–23).

58. Directing the child in the exercise of his or her freedom of thought, conscience and religion is a joint responsibility of both parents. When parents disagree, the matter must be decided on the one hand with regard to the child's autonomous exercise of his or her right in the light of his or her evolving capacities, and on the other hand in the perspective of the best interests of the child (Article 3 CRC).

---

[72] CRC Committee, *Concluding Observations: Norway* (UN Doc. CRC/C/15/Add.126, 2000), paras. 26–27.

[73] *Cf.* The Committee's remarks on the previous system: 'The Committee notes that although an opting-out system exists for children wishing to abstain from compulsory religious education, this requires their parents to submit a formal request exposing the faith of the children involved and as such may be felt to be an infringement of their right to privacy' (CRC Committee, *Concluding Observations: Norway* (UN Doc. CRC/C/15/Add. 23, 1994), para. 9.

59. Article 14(2) obliges the State to ensure that parents and legal guardians exercise their right of direction 'in a manner consistent with the evolving capacities of the child'. This implies that for children with normal mental capacities, the parental power in this respect diminishes, as the child grows older.[74] The State's obligation thus includes the duty to guard the limits of parental direction in matters of religion and conscience, and if necessary to offer protection to children against infringement of their freedom of thought, conscience and religion by their parents.

60. Probably the most difficult situation arises when a child's choice of religion does not coincide with the parents' choice for the child. Very small children obviously do not have the capacity to choose a religion. Hence, parental direction at that stage means amongst other things that parents choose whether or not the child joins a religion, and if so, which religion. Yet a child brought up without a religion may want to join one, and a child brought up within a religion may want to give it up or change it for another religion. If the parents do not agree with this, they can impose their will on their child only until a certain age. Article 14 of the CRC does not indicate at what age a child's 'evolving capacities' have reached the stage at which the child's fundamental choice in matters of religion and conscience must get priority over that of the parents. It is not even clear whether this 'breaking point' must necessarily be situated below the age of 18. Upon ratification, the government of the Netherlands made the following declaration: 'It is the understanding of the Government of the Kingdom of the Netherlands that Article 14 of the Convention is in accordance with the provisions of Article 18 of the International Covenant on Civil and Political Rights of 19 December 1966 and that this article shall include the freedom of a child to have or adopt a religion or belief of his or her choice as soon as the child is capable of making such choice in view of his or her age or maturity.'[75] The fact that the need for this declaration was felt, indicates that at least for this government, the meaning of Article 14 is not clear with regard to the child's freedom of choice in religion. It is indeed not

---

[74] Certain States made reservations, safeguarding 'the primary and inalienable rights of parents' (Holy See) and 'parental authority' (Poland, Kiribati, Singapore).

[75] *Cf.* the interpretative declaration of Belgium: 'The Belgian Government declares that it interprets article 14, paragraph 1, as meaning that, in accordance with the relevant provisions of article 18 of the International Covenant on Civil and Political Rights of 19 December 1966 and article 9 of the European Convention for the Protection of Human Rights and Fundamental Freedoms of 4 November 1950, the right of the child to freedom of thought, conscience and religion implies also the freedom to choose his or her religion or belief.'

necessarily incompatible with the text of Article 14(2) to give priority to parental authority with regard to this most fundamental aspect until the age of majority, while allowing growing child autonomy in matters relating to less fundamental choices, for example regarding the participation in religious education or the observance of certain religious rules (cf. infra, No. 62). The Guidelines for Periodic Reports under Article 1 ask for information on the legal age defined in legislation for choosing a religion or attending religious school teaching.[76] This indicates that in the opinion of the CRC Committee, a right to autonomous choice in religion must be granted below the age of 18. Some States have made legal provisions in this respect. For example, Article 303 of the Swiss Civil Code stipulates that children aged 16 can choose their religion, whereas a German Law from 1921 sets that age at 14.[77]

61. In States where the public school system offers a choice with regard to religious education (for example the possibility to opt out of the religious curriculum, or a choice between courses in different religions and/or a neutral ethics course), this choice cannot be left in the hands of the parents or legal guardians until the child reaches majority. The choice with regard to religious education is less radical than that with regard to the membership of a religion. Hence, the capacity to make a choice with regard to religious education is probably reached sooner than the capacity to make that other, more fundamental choice. The CRC Committee expressed its concern about the situation in Poland, where students require parental consent to attend ethics courses instead of religion courses. Yet in its recommendation, it did not indicate from what age the parental consent requirement should be dropped, referring simply to 'parental direction provided in a manner consistent with the child's evolving capacities'.[78] Different national legislators have made different choices in this matter. For example in Norway (cf. supra, No. 56), children make their own choice from the age of 15. In Poland, secondary schools must introduce a course of religion either at the request of the parents or at that of the 15 to 18-year-old students themselves.[79] In Switzerland and Germany, the same age applies as for the choice of religion, i.e. respectively 16 and 14.

---

[76] CRC Committee, *General Guidelines regarding the form and the contents of the periodic reports* (UN Doc. CRC/C/58, 1996), para. 24.

[77] Gesetz über die religiöse Kindererziehung, 15 July 1921, RGBl. S. 939.

[78] CRC Committee, *Concluding Observations: Poland, o.c.* (note 69), para. 33.

[79] Law on educational system, September 7, 1991 (A. Lopatka, 'Appropriate Direction and Guidance in the Exercise by a Child of the Rights to Freedom of Expression, Thought,

62. Another area in which the capacity to make a choice is probably acquired at a younger age than the capacity to choose a religion as such, is that of the specific way of observing a religion, where this offers a certain leeway. Within one religious community some members may be stricter than others, for example in respecting dietary rules or dress rules. Whereas children will rarely go to court against for example the obligation to wear an Islamic headscarf, this issue may arise in specific contexts, such as when a school provides religion-based exemptions from a general rule prohibiting the wearing of head coverings, or provides special meals to satisfy religious requirements. Applying for an exemption or a special measure of this type will be a task of the parents or legal guardians when young children are concerned, but should at some stage become the child's autonomous right.

63. The manner in which parents and legal guardians exercise their right and duty to give direction in matters of conscience and religion must be consistent with the Convention as a whole.[80] In the decisions they take, the best interests of the child must be a primary consideration (Article 3 CRC). As soon as the child is capable of forming his or her own views, they must give him or her the chance to express those and must give them due weight in accordance with the age and maturity of the child (Article 12(1) CRC). Moreover, in trying to impose their idea, they can never resort to mental or physical violence (Article 19 CRC).

64. An issue that has frequently lead to judicial procedures in domestic law, is that of the refusal of certain types of medical treatment on religious grounds. When parents refuse a treatment for their child, and the child is not capable of expressing his or her own views, their position is weak, since their right is only an accessory right to give direction in the child's exercise of religious freedom. Depending on the medical circumstances of the case, the court must have the power to overrule the parental decision in such a case, in the name of the best interests of the child.[81] When a minor refuses treatment against the wishes of his or her parents, he or she has a stronger position, exercising an autonomous right, but the judge will likewise have to take into account the medical circumstances in deciding according to the child's best interests. This remains the case when the parents and the child agree in their refusal of treatment.

Conscience and Religion', in E. Verhellen (ed.), *Monitoring Children's Rights* (Kluwer Law International 1996), p. 292.

[80] See R. Hodgkin and P. Newell, *o.c.* (note 6), p. 198.

[81] *Ibid.*, p. 199.

4. Para. 3: 'Freedom to manifest one's religion or beliefs may be subject only to such limitations as are prescribed by law and are necessary to protect public safety, order, health, or morals or the fundamental rights and freedoms of others.'

65. The third paragraph of Article 14 is a limitation clause, applicable to the State's negative obligation, i.e. the obligation 'to respect'. Moreover, it applies only to the freedom to manifest one's religion or beliefs, i.e. the external aspect of the rights mentioned in para. 1. The right of parents and legal guardians to provide direction to the child in the exercise of his or her right, protected in para. 2, is not subjected to the limitation clause.

66. Article 14(3) of the CRC is identical to Article 18(3) of the CCPR and Article 12(3) of the CMW and almost identical to Article 12(3) of the ACHR and Article 9(2) of the ECHR. Restrictions are justified if they satisfy three conditions: they must be prescribed by law, they must serve one of the enumerated interests, and they must be necessary to protect that interest. In the CRC, similar limitation clauses exist in Articles 13 and 15.

67. The requirement of a legal basis is to be understood as referring to a general norm, not necessarily an act of Parliament, that is accessible to all citizens and that is sufficiently specific for citizens to be able to foresee its application to their own situation.[82]

68. In its General Comment No. 22 on Article 18 of the CCPR, the Human Rights Committee stressed that 'paragraph 3 of Article 18 is to be strictly interpreted: restrictions are not allowed on grounds not specified there, even if they would be allowed as restrictions to other rights protected in the Covenant, such as national security.[83] Limitations may be applied only for those purposes for which they were prescribed and must be directly related and proportionate to the specific need on which they are predicated. Restrictions may not be imposed for discriminatory purposes or applied in a discriminatory manner.'[84] Regarding the limitation grounds

---

[82] *Cf.* with regard to Article 18 of the CCPR, M. Nowak, *o.c.* (note 3), p. 325.
[83] *Cf.* CRC Committee, *Concluding Observations: Korea* (UN Doc. CRC/C/15/Add.51, 1996), para. 13: The Committee expressed its concern at the insufficient measures adopted to ensure effective implementations of civil rights and fundamental freedoms of children, including freedom of conscience and religion, adding that 'The threats to national security invoked by the Government have hampered the enjoyment of such fundamental freedoms'.
[84] Human Rights Committee, *General Comment No. 22, o.c.* (note 25), para. 8.

included in Article 18(3) of the CCPR (and in Article 14(3) of the CRC), the Human Rights Committee commented only on the ground of the protection of morals: 'The Committee observes that the concept of morals derives from many social, philosophical and religious traditions; consequently, limitations on the freedom to manifest a religion or belief for the purpose of protecting morals must be based on principles not deriving exclusively from a single tradition.'[85] In general the list of limitation grounds is rather restrictive, as is shown in the comparison of the limitation grounds in Article 14(3) of the CRC with those in Articles 13(2) and 15(2) of the CRC. The concept of 'public safety' seems more restricted than that of 'national security'. The two are certainly not synonyms, as is shown by their juxtaposition in Article 15(2) of the CRC. As an example of a restriction of religious freedom in the name of public safety, Nowak mentions the case when during a religious assembly, a specific danger arises threatening the security of persons or things, particularly when hostile religious groups confront one another or when religious customs are made to serve political interests.[86] Moreover, Article 14(3) mentions (public) 'order' as a limitation ground, whereas Articles 13(2) and 15(2) mention 'public order (ordre public)'. Again, this is a restriction, referring more specifically to the prevention of disorder, whereas 'ordre public' includes more abstract protection of societal values, and may be best translated by 'public policy'.[87] Finally, the limitation ground for the protection of the rights and freedoms of others is narrowed to the protection of the 'fundamental' rights and freedoms of others. One may think in this respect of the protection against discrimination or of the religious freedom of others (which may come under pressure if they are put in the minority and the majority aggressively promotes its religion). As an example of the restriction of religious freedom in the name of morals, Nowak mentions certain 'black masses'.[88] An example of the restriction of religious freedom in the name of (public) health is a blood transfusion to save a child's life against the religiously motivated wish of the parents (cf. supra, No. 64), or mandatory vaccination despite contrary religious convictions in the interest of the health of others.[89] Health-based restrictions can also apply to harmful traditional practices that are motivated by religion. Article 5(5) of

---

[85] Ibid.
[86] M. Nowak, o.c. (note 3), pp. 326–327.
[87] Cf. C.D. de Jong, o.c. (note 23) p. 98, quoting a 1951 statement of the Secretary-General of the United Nations, made during the drafting of the CCPR.
[88] M. Nowak, o.c. (note 3), p. 329.
[89] M. Nowak, o.c. (note 3), pp. 328–329.

the Declaration on the Elimination of Religious Intolerance and of Discriminations Based on Religion or Belief provides that 'practices of a religion or beliefs in which a child is brought up must not be injurious to his physical or mental health or to his full development'. An example could be circumcision. Circumcision of boys is in many cases based on religion. An argument can be made that it threatens boys' physical health, in particular through the risks involved in the operation, as well as their psychological health through the consequences of the operation. Circumcision of girls on the other hand, is widely recognized as having negative health effects in a substantial number of cases. Yet this practice is rarely defended on the basis of religious freedom, but rather as a cultural practice. In the CRC, it is more appropriately discussed under Article 24(3), dealing with the need to abolish traditional practices prejudicial to the health of children.[90]

69. Nevertheless, the practice of control bodies under both UN and regional conventions in dealing with limitation clauses shows that when a violation is found, this is almost never based on the finding that the restriction does not further one of the legitimate goals enumerated in the limitation clause. Even if there can be doubts about this aspect, findings of violations are normally based on the argument that the restriction is not proportionate to that goal. Hence, the practical impact of a narrow formulation of limitation grounds as in Article 14(3) of the CRC is limited. Yet the narrow formulation of the limitation grounds in Article 14(3) of the CRC clearly indicates the intention of the drafters to guarantee a strong protection of this right, with only limited restrictions allowed. This should be kept in mind as a guideline when applying the proportionality criterion.

70. Detailed analysis of the proportionality requirement is to be expected mostly on the national level, when legislators implement the CRC, or when judges give it direct effect in domestic law. In the absence of an individual complaint mechanism, the statements of the CRC Committee with regard to specific instances of violations do not leave room for thorough legal analysis. In concluding observations, the Committee states simply: 'the Committee is concerned that restrictions on the freedom to manifest one's religion do not comply with requirements outlined in Article 14, paragraph 3'.[91] In one case it expressed its concern 'that the authorities seem to give

---

[90] Male circumcision may also be discussed under this heading or others, *cf.* J. Smith, 'Male Circumcision and the Rights of the Child', available at www.cirp.org/library/legal/smith/.

[91] CRC Committee, *Concluding Observations: Saudi Arabia, o.c.* (note 16), para. 31; CRC Committee, *Concluding Observations: Uzbekistan, o.c.* (note 16), para. 35: here, the Committee's concern

a wide interpretation to limitations for 'lawful purposes' of the exercise of the rights to freedom of religion, expression and assembly which may prevent the full enjoyment of such rights'.[92] The CRC Committee uses similarly general terms when advising States about the measures they need to take in order to conform to Article 14 of the CRC: It recommends 'that the State Party take effective measures, including enacting or rescinding legislation when necessary, to prevent and eliminate discrimination on the grounds of religion or belief in the recognition, exercise and enjoyment of human rights and fundamental freedoms in all fields of civil, economic, political, social and cultural life',[93] and 'that the State Party make every effort, including public education campaigns, to combat intolerance on the grounds of religion or other belief'.[94] In one case, the Committee endorsed the recommendations made by the Special Rapporteur on the question of religious intolerance following his visit to the State Party and recommended their full implementation.[95]

71. More motivated applications of the limitation clause with regard to the freedom to manifest one's religion can be found in the views of the Human Rights Committee on individual complaints and particularly in the case law of the European Court of Human Rights (as well as the former European Commission of Human Rights). The examples below concern cases that either involve children or that deal with issues that may likely be raised by children.

72. One of the religious prescriptions of the Sikh religion is the wearing of a turban – also by children. This religious rule has lead to legal cases in

relates specifically to Islam and to 'the 1998 Law on Freedom of Conscience and Religious Organizations, and recent amendments to the Civil and Criminal Codes relating to the freedom of religion', yet without indicating which elements of these laws constitute violations of religious freedom; CRC Committee, *Concluding Observations: Iran, o.c.* (note 16), para. 35: here, 'the Committee is especially concerned at the situation of members of non-recognized religions, including the Baha'is, who experience discrimination in areas of, *inter alia*, education, employment, travel, housing and the enjoyment of cultural activities.'

[92] CRC Committee, *Concluding Observations: Indonesia* 1994, *o.c.* (note 49), para. 13.

[93] CRC Committee, *Concluding Observations: Uzbekistan, o.c.* (note 16), para. 36; CRC Committee, *Concluding Observations: Saudi Arabia, o.c.* (note 16), para. 32; CRC Committee, *Concluding Observations: Iran, o.c.* (note 16), para. 36 (slightly different formulation).

[94] CRC Committee, *Concluding Observations: Saudi Arabia, o.c.* (note 16), para. 32; CRC Committee, *Concluding Observations: Iran, o.c.* (note 16), para. 36 (slightly different formulation).

[95] CRC Committee, *Concluding Observations: Iran, o.c.* (note 16), para. 36. This is a rather extensive list of specific proposals for legislative amendments as well as for corrections in the implementation of the laws and in the attitude towards religion in practice: UN Doc. E/CN.4/ 1996/95/Add.2.

several jurisdictions, in particular regarding situations where Sikhs were required to replace the turban with a protective helmet. In 1989, the Human Rights Committee dismissed the complaint of a Canadian Sikh who was discharged from his employment because of his refusal to wear a hard hat during his work. In the eyes of the Committee, the legislation requiring that workers in federal employment be protected from injury and electric shock by the wearing of safety headgear must be seen as 'a limitation that is justified by reference to the grounds laid down in Article 18, paragraph 3'.[96] The European Commission on Human Rights in 1978 ruled inadmissible the complaint of a Sikh man living in the United Kingdom, who had been fined twenty times for failing to wear a crash helmet when riding his motor cycle. Without much motivation, the Commission decided that the interference this caused with his freedom of religion was justified for the protection of health in accordance with Article 9(2) of the ECHR.[97]

73. Successful claims of violation of religious freedom before the European Court of Human Rights are scarce. A significant number of claims are held inadmissible for being manifestly ill founded. The European Court of Human Rights held that the complaint of parents, who were members of the Seventh Day Adventist Church about a refusal to grant their son exemption from Saturday school in conformity with the rules of their religion, was manifestly ill founded.[98] The Court recognized that the refusal constituted an interference with the parents' right to manifest their religion, but ruled that it was a justified restriction for the protection of the child's right to education. The Court gave priority to the interest of the child over that of his parents. However, it might have found the balancing somewhat more difficult if a violation of religious freedom had been invoked also on behalf of the child.

The Court likewise found no violation in the prohibition on students at a Turkish public university to wear an Islamic headscarf.[99] The Court granted a wide margin of appreciation to the national authorities in this matter, arguing that 'where questions concerning the relationship between State and religions are at stake, on which opinion in a democratic society may reasonably differ widely, the role of the national decision-making body must

---

[96] Human Rights Committee, No. 208/1996, *Karnel Singh Binder* v. *Canada*, views of 9 November 1989, para. 6.2.
[97] ECmHR, No. 7992/77, X v. *United Kingdom*, 12 July 1978, *D.R.* 14, p. 234.
[98] ECtHR, *Martins Casimiro and Cerveira Ferreira* v. *Luxemburg*, o.c. (note 32).
[99] ECtHR, *Leyla Şahin* v. *Turkey*, 29 June 2004. This case will be re-examined by a Grand Chamber.

be given special importance'[100], and 'a margin of appreciation is particularly appropriate when it comes to the regulation by the Contracting States of the wearing of religious symbols in teaching institutions, since rules on the subject vary from one country to another depending on national traditions (. . .) and there is no uniform European conception of the requirements of 'the protection of the rights of others' and of 'public order' (. . .).'[101] In the Turkish context, where a very strict interpretation of secularism is a central characteristic of contemporary democracy, and where 'there are extremist political movements (. . .) which seek to impose on society as a whole their religious symbols and conception of a society founded on religious precepts',[102] the ban is in the eyes of the Court a proportionate measure for the protection of the rights and freedoms of others and for the maintenance of public order. In this respect the Court points out 'the impact which wearing such a symbol, which is presented or perceived as a compulsory religious duty, may have on those who choose not to wear it'.[103] Although the applicant in this case was a 24 year-old university student at the time of the facts, there can be little doubt that the European Court of Human Rights would accept a headscarf ban imposed on minor pupils in the same circumstances. Nevertheless, the validity of the European Court's reasoning in the light of Article 14 of the CRC remains doubtful, since the CRC Committee has taken a different stance, expressing its concern with regard to regulations prohibiting the wearing of a headscarf by schoolgirls[104] as well as by their teachers.[105] Commenting on a French law that prohibits the wearing of religious symbols in public schools, the Committee stated: "The dress code of schools may be better addressed within the public schools themselves, encouraging participation of children",[106] thus suggesting a shift from a protective paradigm to a perspective of children's autonomy and participation in this field. The European Court of Human Rights did find a violation in a case involving the criminal conviction of a Jehovah's Witness for proselytism.[107] The judgment is interesting for the distinction it makes between acceptable and unacceptable forms of proselytism, in the

---

[100] *Ibid.*, para. 101.
[101] *Ibid.*, para. 102.
[102] *Ibid.*, para. 109.
[103] *Ibid.*, para. 108.
[104] CRC Committee, *Concluding Observations: Tunisia*, *o.c.* (note 54), para. 29; CRC Committee, *Concluding Observations: France* (UN Doc. CRC/C/15/Add.240, 2004), paras. 25–26.
[105] CRC Committee, *Concluding Observations: Germany*, *o.c.* (note 14), para. 30.
[106] CRC Committee, *Concluding Observations: France*, *o.c.* (note 104), para. 26.
[107] ECtHR, *Kokkinakis* v. *Greece*, 25 May 1993, *Publications of the Court*, Series A, No. 260–A.

evaluation of the proportionality of the restrictive measure with the goal of the protection of the rights of others: 'a distinction has to be made between bearing Christian witness and improper proselytism. The former corresponds to true evangelism, which a report drawn up in 1956 under the auspices of the World Council of Churches describes as an essential mission and a responsibility of every Christian and every Church. The latter represents a corruption or deformation of it. It may, according to the same report, take the form of activities offering material or social advantages with a view to gaining new members for a Church or exerting improper pressure on people in distress or in need; it may even entail the use of violence or brainwashing; more generally, it is not compatible with respect for the freedom of thought, conscience and religion of others'.[108] Hence, this definition delimits the scope of freedom of religion in two respects: the freedom to proselytize is limited by the respect that is due for the freedom of others to be protected against undue pressure in the religious sphere, and vice versa. Depending on the circumstances, a child's freedom of religion may be on either side of the conflict: children may themselves attempt to convert others – for example their fellow pupils in school, or in a youth organisation; and are also a probable target of proselytist activities, both by other children and by adults.

74. In Article 18 of the CCPR, the freedom from coercion to have or to adopt a religion or belief cannot be restricted.[109] Yet since this is based on its formulation in a separate paragraph, which is not found in Article 14 of the CRC, there is no ground to exclude this aspect of religious freedom from the limitation clause of Article 14(3) of the CRC. Nevertheless, one cannot easily imagine a situation in which this type of coercion would be regarded as a proportionate restriction of religious freedom in the name of a legitimate goal.

75. The Human Rights Committee's General Comment No. 22 on Article 18 of the CCPR states that 'persons already subject to certain legitimate constraints, such as prisoners, continue to enjoy their rights to manifest their religion or belief to the fullest extent compatible with the specific nature of the constraint'.[110] This applies also to children who are deprived of their liberty. This has been developed in more detail in the United Nations Rules

---

[108] *Ibid.*, para. 48.
[109] Human Rights Committee, *General Comment No. 22, o.c.* (note 24), para. 8.
[110] Human Rights Committee, *General Comment No. 22, o.c.* (note 24), para. 8.

for the Protection of Juveniles Deprived of their Liberty,[111] which the CRC Committee has commended to States Parties:[112] '(. . .) The religious and cultural beliefs, practices and moral concepts of the juvenile should be respected' (rule 4) and 'Every juvenile should be allowed to satisfy the needs of his or her religious and spiritual life, in particular by attending the services or meetings provided in the detention facility or by conducting his or her own services and having possession of the necessary books or items of religious observance and instruction of his or her denomination. If a detention facility contains a sufficient number of juveniles of a given religion, one or more qualified representatives of that religion should be appointed or approved and allowed to hold regular services and to pay pastoral visits in private to juveniles at their request. Every juvenile should have the right to receive visits from a qualified representative of any religion of his or her choice, as well as the right not to participate in religious services and freely to decline religious education, counselling or indoctrination.' (rule 48)

---

[111] 14 December 1990, UN Doc. A/RES/45/112.
[112] R. Hodgkin and P. Newell, *o.c.* (note 6), p. 202.